THE
SPEAKER'S
EDGE

The Public Speakers A to Z Guide for Turning Your
Part-Time Speaking Hobby Into a Full-Time
Professional Speaking Career on Stage and Online

MICHAEL D. BUTLER

Quantity sales special discounts are available on quantity purchases by corporations, associations, and others. For details, contact the publisher at the address above.

Orders by U.S. trade bookstores and wholesalers.
Email info@ BeyondPublishing.net

The Beyond Publishing Speakers Bureau can bring authors to your live event. For more information or to book an event contact the Beyond Publishing Speakers Bureau speak@BeyondPublishing.net

The Author can be reached directly at BeyondPublishing.net and MichaelDButler.com

Manufactured and printed in the United States of America distributed globally by BeyondPublishing.net

BEYOND
PUBLISHING

New York | Los Angeles | London | Sydney

ISBN Hardcover: 978-1-63792-172-2

ISBN Softcover: 978-1-63792-173-9

Library of Congress Control Number: 2021920116

CONTENTS

INTRODUCTION
MY FIRST SPEECH

MY FIRST SPEECH

I'm Michael D. Butler, and the bright young man you see in the picture above was me, twelve years old, accepting an award for perfect attendance at the sixth grade awards assembly at Ewing Hasell Middle School. My speech was only a few sentences long, yet I had agonized over it for weeks, carefully and fearfully planning my remarks and rehearsing them in my mind. The speech went through more than a couple of drafts.

Until that day, public speaking terrified me. In fact, I was terrified of speaking at all. I stuttered as a kid, and nothing seemed to protect or insulate me from the ridicule and teasing from my classmates or the pitying looks from adults. The sad truth is that I was naturally an outgoing and gregarious kid, but somehow when I entered kindergarten, anxiety seemed to freeze my voice. I stuttered from the age of five until I was eleven. I resigned myself to be a recluse, a weirdo, condemned to suffer in silence.

But then came this three-sentence speech, in which I would accept my award. Something in me was determined to beat the stutter. I would thank my teachers, my classmates, and my principal. I would thank myself for resolving to have perfect attendance. I would thank my mother for getting me on the bus or in the car every morning. I would speak in public, and it would be good.

When I finished, the auditorium filled with thunderous applause. That feeling was amazing.

The next time it happened, I had just delivered a speech on weather forecasting to Mr. Kelley's seventh grade class. The exhilaration of the audience's appreciation went clean through me. At that age, I knew of only two professional speaking careers: meteorologist and minister. Well, I would be one or the other. This was what I wanted to do for the rest of my life. And so, I have.

I wrote this book to be a resource for Toastmasters Groups, the National Speakers Association, and for use in advanced public speaking courses. We will assume you have a certain level of public speaking experience;

that you already understand the importance of diction, projection, rehearsal, eye contact, and all the basics taught in Speech 101 and only touch on these subjects for quick review. We are going to move you forward now, to the next level, and the next, and the next after that – once you gain *The Speaker's Edge*, there is no stopping you.

I wrote this book to prepare you to be the professional public speaker that you believe you can be, to make an impact, make a difference, and change the world.

Chapter One
THE SPEAKER'S EDGE

IF YOU WERE RESTARTING YOUR CAREER TODAY AS A PAID PROFESSIONAL SPEAKER, WHAT WOULD YOU DO DIFFERENTLY?

Picture this.

You feel and hear the rumble of an excited crowd as the emcee introduces you, reading notes from your bio and a list of your credentials. You know you deserve to be here. You've prepared your whole life for this moment. Your nerves still jump to life: your heart rate accelerates, your palms perspire. But now you know these are just signs of excitement and anticipation.

You think back to that first speech you labored through just two years ago. How different things were back then. And you are grateful to have invested in yourself, your business, and your future.

You peek through the curtain. The event planner was right: there is not an empty seat in the venue. .

You hear your name and then, the eruption of applause. Heart pounding, you take the stage, grabbing the mic, radiating confidence. For the next 45 minutes, you land your message like a sharp arrow bursting through the center ring of the target, thrilling your audience with life-changing, transformational content.

When you finish, a throng of raving fans rushes back to

your book table to buy your book, to ask for your autograph on the inside page, maybe even to get a selfie with you, so they can prove to their friends that they met you. It's exactly this moment you realize just how much your hard work, belief in yourself, and investment in your speaking career paid off.

CAN YOU SEE IT? CAN YOU HEAR THEM?

Your audience will never be the same. And tomorrow, you will make an even bigger impact.

WHAT IS THE SPEAKER'S EDGE?

We know when someone has *The Speaker's Edge*. Even more, we know when they don't. We've all agonized for a speaker who suffered getting through their presentation. It might have been a teacher, pastor, coach, or even a "professional". They needed feedback and weren't getting it. They needed finesse and weren't finding it. They had the data, but their message got lost. Things were awkward, distracting, distressing, or simply boring.

Speakers with the Edge speak not from just the head, but from the heart. They are masters at reading their audience and making split-second shifts and lightning-speed calculations for maximum impact of their points.

Very few people succeed on stage, but if you are committed and determined, if you can stand in the center of the arena through sixty seconds of silence, you have the strength and the fortitude to take those individuals anywhere you want them to go.

Think of a time when you spoke onstage and there was fear. I'm thinking of a time when I was eight years old in the third grade. In the spelling bee, I stood up and misspelled a word. It brought back a lot of my fear of stuttering. Think of a time when you were called on to speak for the first time – how did you feel? Were you nervous, anxious? Did you feel inadequate? Embarrassed or "less than"? Hold that picture in your mind, because you're about to release that image and forgive yourself for not sticking up for yourself. Forgive yourself for letting people run over you.

Why do you want to be a public speaker? To make a difference in the world? To increase new clients? To sell books? To establish credibility? Take a few minutes and write down the reason.

Are you committed to doing the work that it takes to get there? A few years ago, I ran my first marathon. It took six months of training, but that wasn't the most important factor. I had to have the determination. Those who are committed to their craft go from being five-figure speakers to seven or even eight-figure speakers. Some people might say they're not in it for the money, and that's fine, but never assume that speaking for free automatically makes it a noble cause. The money matters. The money proves that you are making an impact. If your message is a valuable one, it may even be selfish to play it small. Step out there and take command of your value.

The Speaker's Edge is the power to persuade and move an audience. If you can make an audience cry or laugh, that's amazing. But if you can convince your audience to make life-changing decisions: be healthier, be kinder, be a better spouse or parent? Those are the things that make an eternal difference in the life of that person, and in the lives of everyone around them. A great speaker can motivate people to make decisions and change their life for the better.

There is a way to move beyond being "speaking in public" to "public speaking" to "professional speaker". It comes from inside you, yet it is a force so powerful that everyone can see it.

Les Brown is a personal hero of mine; I guess he's a hero to a lot of people. He came out of a background where he was labeled, marginalized, and discouraged, and through his own determination and hard work, became a vastly influential motivational speaker, radio DJ, TV personality, author, and even a member of the Ohio House of Representatives for several years.

I remember him telling the stories of his early days of corporate engagement speaking, when nobody really knew who he was. He spent hours studying the company he was going to speak for. He did the research, asked questions of the event planner, the vice president and president of that company, talked to anybody he could find who could tell him something of value. He learned what the company was going through, who they were listening to, and who they had in to speak during the previous years. Based on what was happening in the company right then, he found stories in the media, stories from history, salient points that he could apply to his talk. He might have always been giving the same core keynote elements, but he would drive home his point based on what was relevant to that audience. He went the extra mile.

A great speaker – a speaker with the Edge - goes that extra mile. That can be you.

You understand that public speaking starts before you ever step in front of the audience and continues long after you've left the stage. You know your audience, know your topic. You exude trust, empathy, humor, and understanding. You show up early and check out the room, check for adequate lighting, make sure that the temperature is comfortable, that the audio-visual setup is correct, even that the restrooms are clean and well-stocked, the catering table is ready, and the event planner is steady on his or her feet.

For example, if you show up early and the event planner is overwhelmed, ask how you can help. A lot of times, if they're understaffed, you might even help move chairs. Never be too proud to move a chair – the goodwill you create will come back tenfold. *The Speaker's Edge* makes you go above and beyond – even if the venue is running late and you only get 35 minutes, instead of 55 minutes. When you finish, you follow up, accept feedback with grace, and know that there are always ways to improve. Mistakes and misfires are nothing more than learning experiences.

The Speaker's Edge is the knowledge that there is more to great public speaking than simply having a great speech – and in that understanding, a great speech becomes unforgettable.

Chapter 2
FINDING YOUR VOICE

EVERY CHILD IS BORN A GENIUS

It would be wonderful if we were all raised in environments that encouraged us from an early age to speak our minds, to appreciate our own strengths and personalities, and to know that our words mattered. If we had been given guidance and correction not by stifling our words, but by open communication, so we could learn by example and understand that adults were not discounting us but mentoring us, that they were showing us the path to becoming who we really are, instead of the someone else's idea of who we should be. If you were lucky enough to have been raised in a home or given an education like this, that is wonderful, and I hope that you pass those skills on to your children, or employees, or whomever is looking to you for cues and support.

But many of us were held to a different standard – the notion that children should be seen, and not heard. The idea that we were meant to be behave a certain way or become a certain thing. The pressure to conform. The demands to meet someone else's idea of perfection or impressiveness.

Does this sound familiar? Your entire life, you've been told to be quiet. You have lived with the fear of disobeying, the fear of offending, the fear of being sat down, singled out, punished for speaking up or speaking out. As newborns we used our cries to meet our needs – hopefully – but at some point in our lives, we lose our voice. We're told many times to be quiet, to not speak, told to "listen up" and bite our tongue. Maybe it's a parent, a teacher, a sibling, classmates, a coach, or a pastor. Too many times, we internalize "be quiet" and apply the meaning: "my voice does not matter." We are told to color inside the lines and told to be quiet. Many children stop thinking logically at this point, we adopt "group think," we comply, so we'll fit in and not be publicly shamed.

Perhaps you're from a large family and your voice was seldom heard. Perhaps somewhere in your education, you realized your voice did not matter or was not "normal" enough to be accepted (or worse, it resulted in torment, bullying, or shame), so you stopped trying. Withdrawing into silence is a defense mechanism. If you stop speaking, your words cannot be used against you.

What if you could find your voice? Not just your outside powerful and loud voice, but your inside voice with strength, confidence, and courage? What if you could speak confidently and boldly, even with your inside voice?

There's something fearful about finding your voice. The idea of speaking your ideas aloud sounds radical, even dangerous. When you finally find your voice, it can be a guilty pleasure of emotions, realizing your power and potential for the first time since crying as a newborn.

I'M HERE TO HELP YOU FIND YOUR VOICE

Or in this case, re-find it and re-claim it. Yes, that divine spark that is alive on the inside of every human, laced there by God himself before you were even born. That unique thumbprint that makes up "you", just waiting to be discovered, so you can leave your eternal mark on the world. The legacy "brand" you will be known and remembered for. Your signature talk, your signature keynote, your signature workshop, your signature impact!

Sounds like a big job, right? It is, but I believe you are up for it. And it's easier than you might think. You were born for this. You never lost your ability to command a room. I'm about to reconnect you with you. I'm about to reconnect you with the power of your voice and give you back what was yours all along: the power to influence, impact, and inspire with your very own voice.

It's not by accident you are holding this book in your hands. You may even be hiding it from your family and friends because you've secretly had a dream. You've had the dream of being on stage and inspiring a crowd. The fact that you invested in yourself means you know you were born for more, and if this book does not live up to your expectations, I'll personally refund your money.

It doesn't matter if you're an informational speaker, motivational speaker, inspirational speaker, or a transformational speaker. *The Speaker's Edge* can put you on bigger stages and help you launch some of your own stages, but it's all up to you.

THE PAINFUL PROCESS TO FINDING YOUR VOICE

If you've ever lost your voice to laryngitis or some other ailment, you know the frustration of being unable to communicate, even the feeling of fear that you may have lost your voice forever. Short of learning sign language or having the technology to communicate like those who've been disabled in car accidents or a stroke and having to completely learn how to speak again, not being able to communicate your thoughts, feelings, dreams, and message to the world is scary.

But sometimes, it takes a tragedy to truly find your voice. I'm not wishing tragedy upon anyone, but when you study the great speakers of the past 200 years, you realize that many of them found their voice in the midst of extreme crisis, personal pain, and deep, heart-wrenching, soul searching. Speakers who have overcome great adversity of their own reach out to audiences and make a connection because they have been there. They have suffered their own setbacks and come through to let us know that we, too, can conquer adversity.

Here are just a few examples, and this list by no means includes every amazing, powerful public speaker:

- Do you know what Winston Churchill, James Earl Jones, King George IV, Nicole Kidman, Joe Biden, Bruce Willis, Julia Roberts, Michael Phelps, Bill Walton, and Tiger Woods have in common? Each of them struggled with stuttering during some point in their lives.

- Marc Elliot has taken his message to tens of thousands of individuals, despite suffering Tourette's syndrome.

- Autism activist Temple Grandin takes her message on minds that "work differently" before audiences around the world.

- Despite living with cerebral palsy, speakers like John Quinn, Michael Bortolotto, and Mike Berkson and his associate Tim Wambach challenge their audiences with their messages of living to our full potential.

Some of the greatest public speakers were considered very unlikely to succeed on stage. People like Les Brown, Zig Ziglar, Joyce Meyer, Mel Robbins, people like me, even, usually have to work hard to become public speakers. There are so many examples of this. Aimee Semple McPherson was one of the greatest communicators of the century. In the 1920s, she started the first FM radio station in America. She had the largest church congregation in America. As a single woman and a single mother, she had a powerful voice and was greatly respected. But she was not born a "great" orator. She learned how to become a great speaker.

Our top speaker makes $80,000 an hour. His name is Jim Stovall. He owns the Narrative Television Network. He has excelled as a speaker. He's a part of the National Speaker's Association. He's mentored young speakers and has endorsed me as a speaker's coach and as a publisher.

He's also blind. He lost his sight when he was still a young man in college. He went to hear the great Ray Charles play the piano, to inspire himself as to what he could do as a blind man. He took up power lifting to compete in the Olympics.

Jim was attending a support group for the newly blind or those who were going blind, and he heard the complaint, "How can blind people watch TV? I enjoy watching movies, but since I'm going blind, I'm a little depressed that I won't know what's happening on the screen." There was a blind attorney there who said, "Why don't we do something about it? Why don't we start a company?" Together, they started a company together called the Narrative Television Network.

WHO ARE YOU LISTENING TO NOW?

I'm an avid listener of podcasts. I like podcasts because it's niched content on demand. When I'm in the car, at the gym, or even doing my grocery shopping, I can listen to my favorite podcast and get valuable information or get motivated. Podcasts have grown 2,000 percent in the past three years. Eighty percent of Americans have listened to a podcast. If I looked at your phone to see what podcasts you subscribe to, I can predict your success as a speaker and how much you'll be making as a professional speaker three years from now. Along with many others in personal development in the 80s and 90s, I said that we could determine your success by the books that you read and the friends you hang out with, and it's true. It's true with books and friends, and it's true with podcasts.

Who are the people you want to speak to and sell books to listening to right now? What are the conversations they are having online and in person? Once you've identified who the influencers are in the space you want to be the next leader, find out who they are following. Who are the mentors of your mentors? This will give you a clue as to where you need to go.

If you were to launch a podcast, what would the topic be? What would the title be? What would be the goal of your podcast? The reason I'm asking these questions is what you like to listen to and what you like to think about is what you'll be speaking about. Why not move your speaking career in the direction of your dreams, your expertise, and your value?

FIND YOUR VOICE AND TAKE OWNERSHIP OF YOUR LIFE

The voice inside your head is the most important. Really, it's the voice deep inside our heart, our spirit. If you've ever had a "gut feeling" about something that's the inner you trying to guide your mind and body to make the right decision.

That's the voice we need to come out on stage with. That's the voice the world is waiting to hear. The voice in your heart, speaking to your head every day, trying to get you to take action in the direction of your destiny, that is the voice the world desperately needs to hear! As you boldly step into this voice, you will grow in confidence, boldness, and faith, and it will soon become second nature for you to have this confidence. The more comfortable you are speaking from your heart and not just your head, the more effective you will be.

When I talk about speaking from your heart, I'm talking about speaking from your passion, from your core values, from your inner being. If you can transition from speaking from your head to your heart, and then reach out and speak to other peoples' hearts, this is where you can make the most impact!

When I talk about speaking from the heart, obviously I'm not talking about your heart as the physical organ that pumps blood. I'm talking about speaking to their core. Speak to that God-like person on the inside of them that they are and their core values. Their spirit is seeking to grow, to expand, and to be communicated with. They are ready to unleash their inner greatness, but only when you give them permission from stage. Once you accept this challenge, you'll realize that public speaking is not just sound waves floating through the air, but it's a transfer of energy. It's an infusion of belief that you have for your audience; you are imparting confidence, strength, and the will and ability to succeed.

INNER PROGRAMMING

There are many opportunities for negativity in life. But I must say I was programmed well.

The first five years of a child's life are the most crucial to receive love, affection, affirmation, and confidence. If a child does not receive an adequate dose of these ingredients, confidence in public speaking will be missing.

This lack of confidence cannot be made up for by

speaking louder on stage or being more forceful on stage. The kind of confidence present in the most successful public speakers does not require raising the voice to get noticed, but can be communicated in a quiet and even soft tone with great authority and resolve.

Fortunately for me, I was brought up in a structured and strict home. My brother and I were required to do our chores and finish our homework before we could watch TV in the evening. And if we had to study for a test, there was no TV at all. These strict rules in our home helped us develop self-discipline that helped us succeed in life.

Not only did we have this strong influence from both parents, but we also had a strong faith-based upbringing that instilled confidence and courage in us. We were taught that we were born for something great and that we could make a difference in the world, and we believed it.

I remember a list of positive affirmations I got a hold of at about the age of 11. I'd say these positive affirmations every day in front of the mirror before I went to school for almost an entire year. I remember this had a huge impact on my emotional health, my confidence level, and my self-esteem. As a boy who stuttered and didn't feel confident on most days, this exercise helped make the difference for what I needed in my life.

If you were not programmed well—and let's face it: all

of us could have received more love, encouragement, and confidence—the world is a tough place, and any time you strike out to do something to help others like speaking on stage, you'll be faced with obstacles, setbacks, criticism, and negativity. It's hard for some speakers to begin speaking from the heart because they've done business in their head for years, and that's the way they've always been wired.

It's not too late to reprogram yourself for success.

1. Change your self-talk. No more deep personal criticism or self-doubt. Reprogram the way you think about yourself. I want you to look at yourself in the mirror every day and tell yourself the following affirmations:

a. I am more than enough.

b. I am loved.

c. I am confident.

d. I am capable.

e. I am powerful.

f. I am kind.

g. I am courageous.

h. I deserve more.

i. I deserve love.

When my mentor had me say these things to myself on my way to door-to-door sales calls, they changed my life – because saying that you like yourself prior to entering a sales situation immediately improves your chances of success. Say them a thousand times, and then say them a thousand times more. They will go from being words you simply hear in your ears to powerful beliefs in your subconscious, energizing you to action. Reprogramming your self-image is an essential part of your success.

2. Change who you are listening to. Cut yourself off from negativity. If the negativity is coming from a source you cannot simply "cut off" (a parent, your spouse, your boss), then either have serious discussion with that person, making it clear that you will no longer tolerate the behavior, or – and this may be an even greater victory – just learn to ignore them. Some people cannot be changed, but you can change the way they affect you. If they are wrong, stop believing or caring what they say. They'll get the idea soon enough that their power over you is gone.

3. Now combine Number 1 and Number 2, and take your changed inner beliefs about yourself and state out loud, in your words and actions, who you are, what you believe, and what you are called to do!

Imagine walking into a room where you were confident and secure in the fact that your message will be heard and that your message will be respected. Would that calm you down? How would you feel if you knew that not only are you being heard today, but you are also being respected? Imagine walking into a room where you commanded the utmost respect, honor, and highest esteem. Everyone in the room is leaning forward to listen to you and is hanging on every word you say.

With mentoring and encouragement, anyone has the power to make this happen. This is the reason I designed the course Speak Better in 60 Days. This is the reason I wrote *The Speaker's Edge*, and the reason I launched Global Elite Speaker's Bureau. Because the sky is the limit.

EDGY EXERCISE #1

Make a list of your top ten speakers you like to listen to on a regular basis.

It can be a podcaster, a pastor, a TV preacher, a TedTalk—it doesn't matter what kind of speaker they are.

Make a list of your top ten favorite speakers, and tell me why they are your favorites:

1)_____ because _____

2)_____ because _____

3)_____ because _____

4)_____ because _____

5)_____ because _____

6)_____ because _____

7)_____ because _____

8)_____ because _____

9)_____ because _____

10)_____ because _____

Chapter 3
BETTER COMMUNICATION

And right off the bat, we're deep into the weeds. I could write twenty books on "communication" and never come close to covering the entire subject. Our world, our species, depends on so many different forms of communication that we might as well go back to the Stone Age to begin. The truth is, you as a human being already know intuitively just about everything you need to know about communicating. It's hardwired into you. Within your first days on Earth, you realized that your voice could get you what you wanted. A crying baby makes 98 percent of adults take action: find a binkie, bring a diaper or a bottle, pick the baby up and soothe it. Voices are hardwired to move us; we are hardwired to use them.

- The question is not how to communicate; it's how to communicate better.

- First and foremost, better communication doesn't just happen.

- It requires an effort.

I believe that, as a people, we are generally worse communicators today than we were twenty or even ten years ago. The Internet has brought us together in many ways, yet in other ways, it has shortened our attention spans, especially in Millennials and Gen Z. Because they have grown up on devices, it is simply what they are accustomed to. It's not at all unusual at a restaurant to see a family seated together with each of them looking down at their own phone, rather than interacting with one another.

Social media takes a great deal of blame for distracting us from face-to-face communication, but when we use social media, it is a choice and doesn't necessarily lead to poor interpersonal communication. Social media platforms can actually be a great tool for communication if used properly, not as a substitute for communication, but as an enhancement of communication. It's a positive way for quick, up-to-the moment status checks for both business and family affairs.

We're not doomed to become tech-obsessed islands unto ourselves. Overall, those who consciously choose to be better communicators, to put down their phones, to respect one another and be in the moment, can do so. When we give those around us the ability to be heard, to give feedback, and to hear us, we all improve.

IMPROVING YOUR ABILITY TO COMMUNICATE

I have always felt that women are naturally better communicators than men. The ability to communicate seems to be a basic tenet of their lives. They express themselves more verbally; they're more predisposed toward it. In my life, the women I know are certainly better communicators. So, how can a man or a woman learn to be a better communicator? By listening more, by communicating more directly, by stating what we want and need, and if we can learn how to communicate in the present (without dwelling on the past), communicating healthy emotional things.

The ability to communicate effectively relies a great deal on common sense and simple etiquette. Treating everyone with respect and equality, knowing your audience, and basic politeness will go a long way toward making you a great communicator. For more professional encounters, note-taking and follow-up to confirm understanding will help you avoid mistakes or misunderstandings.

THE MECHANICS OF SPEAKING

When you say you have three points, make sure you have an introduction and three good points. Then, remind them what the three points were during the conclusion. Those are the mechanics of public speaking. Pitch, tone, inflection, pausing and pacing, eye contact. Points that are clarified and well-demonstrated and brought home to the audience with proper application and a call to action.

Did you know 85 percent of communication is non-verbal?

To leave out the mechanics means leaving out one of the basic elements, like a piece of a jigsaw puzzle or putting a car together – if you have parts left over on the garage floor, you may have a disastrous outing. So it is with a speech. People don't want to feel like they're dangling, hanging in the air. That is why great speeches make and repeat their points, even though it may seem redundant, like so:

Introduction: Tell them what you're going to tell them

Body: Tell them

Conclusion: Tell them what you told them

THE POWER OF LISTENING

All great communicators are first and foremost great listeners. In fact, real communication is impossible without a receptor. Someone has to hear a message for it to have any significance. Great communicators don't just talk nonstop to a fawning audience; they react, respond, and reap the rewards: socially, spiritually, financially, neurologically. If you expect to do well in any organization or in relationships, becoming a better listener will clear the path for you.

We all know people who are great listeners – they are people we want to speak with because they actively listen to what we say and respond appropriately, helpfully, or at least supportively. Even more obvious to us are bad listeners. They fidget, glance away at their phone or whatever shiny object has caught their attention, they may interrupt with, "I know what you're going to say…" or "The same thing happened to me, but like this..." and they somehow manage to make your words all about them. In fact, their responses are so unhelpful and off-topic that you know they haven't heard a word you've said. While you're speaking, they're just planning what they're going to say next, because, to them, their words are so much more interesting than yours.

You know how awful that feels – now don't be that person. Practice attentive listening when someone speaks to you. This means taking the time and effort to focus on not only their words, but their tone and body language. There is no such thing as a boring person, and showing curiosity and interest in what someone has to say invites even greater communication. The more willing you are to listen, the more interesting people become, because they feel they can rely on you to respect their words and feelings.

Are you a good listener? You may think so, but give yourself a little test. The next time you have a conversation with someone, ask yourself some questions afterward. What did you learn about the person? What was on his mind – was something troubling him? What did he want to share? Did you allow him to do so? How do you think he felt about your talk? If you can answer those questions honestly, you were being an attentive listener.

Being a good listener can bring you referrals and new clients.

Remember that listening to someone doesn't require agreement with them. We have a natural instinct to withdraw from opinions that do not match our own, but shutting down when an opposing viewpoint pops up means that you'll miss a chance at greater understanding. If you are solid and secure in your beliefs, listening to opposing or different beliefs should cause you no great distress.

Great listeners are also able to listen without jumping to conclusions or making judgments. If you want to be trusted with real, honest communication, you cannot let personal, knee-jerk judgments cloud your ability to hear what they are saying.

Active, attentive listening has so many benefits that it is shocking how many people are really bad at it – but we live in an age of distractions and self-focused behaviors, a selfie nation eager to tell the rest of the world about their own thoughts, but unwilling to share in the process. But turn your attention outward and listen, because:

- It makes people like you. Have you ever known a great listener that you disliked?

- People will share more information with those they feel are listening to them.

- You learn things – both in a friendly way, and in the deep, neurological sense that new neural pathways form when you make a connection with another human.

- It strengthens relationships. Relationships without attentive listening tend to disintegrate.

- Listening makes you funnier. You can't crack a great joke if you haven't been paying attention to what's going on.

- The job market demands good communicators and collaborators.

- With active listening, you can respond with rationale and helpfulness.

- You are aware of oncoming sources of tension or stress and can diffuse these things proactively, rather than simply reacting to something that has already passed you by.

Here's a fun way to improve listening skills: improvisational comedy. This game requires participants to listen to each other intensely and respond appropriately, due to the completely unpredictable nature of the game. Some corporations are even using improvisational comedy classes to help their teams learn better communication skills.

Chapter 4

PUBLIC AND PROFESSIONAL SPEAKING

WHAT DOES YOUR FUTURE SELF LOOK LIKE?

There are several ways to be employed as a paid public speaker. You can go to work for a speakers' agency, where they fly you around the country to speak about "Topic A" because you are an expert in that space. Or you can go speak for yourself as a hired gun, making $5,000 an hour, speaking on diversity, inclusion, employee engagement, customer retention, customer service, or just being a motivational speaker in a corporate environment.

HOW ARE INTERPERSONAL AND PROFESSIONAL COMMUNICATION ALIKE?

They're alike in the fact that politeness and respect apply to both – if I'm at church, a civic organization, a Toastmaster's group, a networking group, a family reunion, or a wedding, it's a social situation that requires a certain amount of etiquette. It requires listening, asking questions, not always talking about oneself, being polite, and acknowledging who the host is. If I'm called upon to speak, it also requires that I watch the time and that I'm respectful of the time they give me. Kindness 101 and Etiquette 101 are the main rules.

INVESTING IN YOUR SPEAKING SKILLS

The great speakers throughout the decades and around the world weren't born that way. The craft is practiced and studied. They were mentored, coached, and taught by masters. The laws of communication are the same, no matter what your format:

1. Making your message understood.

2. Confidence in yourself. You are the expert.

3. You know why you are there.

4. Knowing your space.

5. Anticipating what rejections and rebuttals will come and countering them.

6. Answering the doubt in your audience's mind before they know it is there.

7. Creating a clear, secure path to drive your point home.

I don't believe there is such a thing as a "natural" public speaker. I think that others will see potential in someone, or that person will have to find the potential in themselves, to nurture the ability to speak and lead, and encourage them in their gifts. I, myself, had pastors encourage me to public speaking when I was young, bringing me onstage to tell a story or read a scripture, to encourage me in my speaking. We can all choose to focus on becoming better – in fact, my course Speak Better in 60 Days is an eight-part course, and someone can go through it in eight weeks, eight days, or even eight hours if they wanted, going from concept to completion and becoming a much better speaker.

Communication is so important in every area and aspect of life. It is the difference between being a five-figure, six-figure, or seven-figure insurance agent, realtor, mortgage lender, or business owner. To be taken seriously, the most effective coaches, actors, and politicians have learned how to be good communicators.

The basic difference in public and professional speaking is that, for professional speaking, you're getting a check. You're actually getting paid to speak on stage (or to be able to communicate effectively on the job, in a more general sense). If you're not getting paid directly, then you're selling to the audience, and it's based on you collecting a check at the back of the room when you're done.

But let's say that I'm brought onto a sales team at a car dealership as a commissioned salesperson. There, I am also a paid public speaker. But what I have to realize in that job position is that, before I can sell anybody a car or make a commission, I must learn to become a good listener; I've got to learn how to become somebody who really understands my customer and what they want; I must establish trust with that customer for them to become a paying customer from whom I'll earn a commission.

In fact, if you want to get mentored in public speaking, I recommend taking a sales job, whether you're going door to door, doing phone sales, or doing commissioned-based sales on a car lot or in a furniture store.

One of my Beyond Publishing authors, Tucker Bearden, is a terrific case in support of this idea. Tucker can sell $2,000 Kirby vacuum cleaners door-to-door in the snow-covered streets of Detroit, Michigan. He is one of the top Kirby sales guys in America.

He grew up raising horses in Arkansas, which landed him a job at the Kentucky Derby, living in the stables with the horses, training and caring for the quarter horses. Eventually, he even had some of his own horses run in the Kentucky Derby. We're actually doing a Kentucky Derby event together this year and next year, to helps rescue kids from human trafficking. He'll be speaking at that, and we will launch his book at that event as well. I was there with Tucker on stage in Vegas a few years ago when he did his first public speech. We've got it on video, and we're going to feature that. He's got a remarkable story, because he, too, grew up with a stutter. He has Asperger's Syndrome, so he's a high-functioning Asperger's advocate who is a certified coach and trainer under Zig Ziglar.

He's really grown a lot in the last four years. I'm so proud of him.

IMPROVING PUBLIC SPEAKING SKILLS

Let's do a quick review from Speech 101. There are four general types or purposes of public speaking: ceremonial, informative, persuasive, and entertaining. From there, the possibilities are endless, and there are countless types of venues. There are keynote speeches, toasts, company meetings, public seminars, client/prospect events, workshops, emceeing or hosting events, subject matter expertise, entertainers, newscasters, debate participants or moderators, and teachers and lecturers. You need not have a formal meeting or gathering set up to be suddenly required to speak to a group. At work or at home, at a moment's notice, you might need to make yourself heard.

There is hardly a job out there that does not require communication skills if you want to do it right, or that does not demand your communication skills improve if you want to do better today than you did yesterday. But no matter who you are or how much experience you have with communicating, there is always a way to better your skills. If you're early in the process, let me offer a few suggestions that will kickstart awareness of your own speaking style.

1.Speak to yourself in the mirror. Be affirmative! Encourage yourself. I know it sounds like that Stuart Smalley bit from Saturday Night Live. But old Stuart wasn't wrong – talking some sense to yourself makes you aware of your sentences and increases your confidence.

2.Record yourself speaking (more than once, so you can check for improvements!).

a. The first goal here is to get used to the sound of your own voice. We hear our voices through the sound-altering dimensions of our own skulls (basically you always hear yourself through a small dome of bone and tissue), so your "out of head" voice will sound odd to you. I'm sure you've heard people say this before, "I sound so weird!" or "I hate the sound of my own voice!" No, you're just not used to hearing it the way everyone else hears it.

b. The second goal is to listen for your bad habits. You're listening for the "ums" and the "uhs" of course, but also for things like words you use way too much. Do you say "basically" or "actually" before most of your sentences? Do you say "y'know," or "amazing", or "okay" a lot? Do you finish your sentences definitively, or do you trail off, or supplement endings of sentences with "so, anyway..." Listen to yourself, and compare the way you speak to the way that a news anchor or a politician would speak, if need be, but chances are, if you're making those kinds of errors, you'll hear them right away. Then, practice speaking without using those crutches.

3.Learn to use more words. A great way to do this is by reading, playing word games, crossword puzzles, anything that opens you up to the vast and beautiful variety of your language.

4.Just speak more in general. Find opportunities to talk with friends, family, associates. Be mentally present when you are speaking with people, and let them speak back to you. You can learn so much by listening to others.

5.Get feedback. If you have to give presentations at work, then ask questions, ask for feedback. Ask your boss and your coworkers how you did, what you did well, and what could have been better or clearer. People are typically happy to give you feedback. And remember to take feedback graciously and, if necessary, with a grain of salt. Just because Jim says he doesn't understand a point that you made – well, okay, that's something to check on, but if there's no real improvement, it may just be Jim's problem. Now if Jim, Jules, Jeff, Joan, and Janette all say it, then heads-up, you need to really examine how you're speaking.

Now let's move beyond merely getting comfortable with speaking and discuss speaking purposefully before an audience. My first advice here is to start small. It's better for you, and it's only practical anyway; without much experience, it's rather unlikely that you'll gather a big audience straightaway. Zoom a talk to five people and see how it goes. Talk to a room of 25 people before you tackle a room of 100. Talk to 100 before you try for 500. You see how this works. As far as practice goes, speaking to 25 people can teach you as much as speaking to 25,000.

Here are some pointers on speaking to a group that will improve your connection to the audience and keep the audience's attention where it should be: on you!

1.Eye Contact. Use the techniques of eye contact with two people on either side of the room. Find someone who is really paying attention and speak to them. Then, find someone on the other side of the room who is really paying attention, and speak to them.

2.Pausing and Pacing.

3.Anchoring. "Anchoring" is when you establish a particular point on the stage that returns focus every time you are there. For example, stand at a corner of the stage and every time you do something positive about buying your program, stand in the same spot, and make the same gesture.

4.Recapturing Control of the Room. One great secret I've learned and used over the years has come from speaking to high school and junior high school students at assemblies. They can be very unruly, and you have no ability to discipline them. But when you walk through the crowd, speaking at a certain volume, then get really quiet, and touch someone on the shoulder, the eyes of everyone in the auditorium go to the person you're touching as they're trying to figure out why you're touching that person on the shoulder, and what you might be saying to them. All you're doing is taking the attention in the room away from the troublemakers into another part of the room. It's a very subtle but effective technique.

5.Never give up the microphone. Only surrender the microphone to the host. If you bring someone up from the audience keep your hand on the microphone and DO NOT ever let someone take the mic from you.

I go into more detail in my course

SpeakBetter60Days.com

Chapter 5
FEAR, ITSELF

THE SECOND-MOST FEARED THING IN THE WORLD IS PUBLIC SPEAKING, SURPASSED ONLY BY THE FEAR OF DEATH.

I can remember the fear and excitement and the adrenaline rush I would get doing door to door sales in Tennessee and Arkansas, when my kids were young and I was out there knocking on doors to put groceries on the table. I had a memorized pitch that I did, and I had to remember how that shaped and molded me into the man I am today.

It all goes back to the first person to help me with public speaking. That was my mother. Because I had run an ad in the newspaper as a 15-year-old kid, I had gotten fourteen lawnmowing jobs. I didn't have a driver's license yet, so I had to save money to buy a lawnmower, and so I had to hire a driver to take me to my lawnmowing jobs.

If it was raining, Mom would make me call Mrs. Jones and Mrs. Smith and tell them I wasn't coming to mow, that I would come tomorrow. I said, "Mom, I don't want to!".

I didn't like talking on the phone. We had a party line growing up in the country in Oklahoma, and there would always be the neighbors on there, gossiping. One of the things my brother and I did for entertainment was just kind of listen in on those stupid conversations. For whatever reason, probably because of my stutter, I didn't want to talk on the phone. For me, talking on the phone was the same as standing in front of a room full of people I didn't know.

But my mom helped me overcome that fear. She made me excel in customer service as a 15-year-old. If they'd had Yelp back then, I would have gotten five stars. But I have to say thanks to my mom for making me pick up the phone. In dialing for dollars, I made millions of dollars over the years, because she helped me overcome the fear of talking on the phone.

STAGE FRIGHT

From being called on by the teacher to read aloud in a grade school classroom to giving your first speech in English class, eventually, every one of us will be called upon to speak in public. It's a part of life and essential for success. Confidence in speaking is something you're born with. Most babies make quite a loud entrance into the world, but at some point, we learn life is safer if we keep our voice down. For many of us, the true fear of public speaking comes from a fear of rejection, a fear of abandonment, and a fear of not being heard.

Every athlete, every speaker, every company president, every politician has that moment with butterflies in their stomach and a lump in their throat and sweaty palms.

They feel the fear and do it anyway. Nerves do not have

to mean you are "bad" at what you're doing, or unprepared, and you should not let the fact that you are nervous upset you. Consider, instead, that your nervousness implies that the speech is important to you, that you care about your topic and your audience. Embrace nervousness as a vital part of the process. That is adrenaline, surging inside you, ready to make you all the more dynamic and persuasive.

If someone has a genuine speaking phobia, they might want to consider another job other than being a professional speaker, but there are things you can do to learn how to manage it well. For example:

- Lessen the amount of time that you actually have to speak during a presentation. This can be accomplished in a few different ways:

  o Calling on others to help with portions of the speech. For example, you might call on Beth or Tom or Susan to give part of the presentation – Tom can give the sales report, Becky can give the report on what she's working on. By calling on others, it takes some pressure off the primary speaker.

  o Interviews. The interview style is very powerful, and if you focus well on your subject, it is more like having a personal conversation than a public speaking engagement. When interviewing a subject, your tone should not be preachy, loud, badgering, bullying, or nagging. Your tone should be, "I like you. I want to hear what you have to say." If you are the subject of the interview, take the tone of "I am the expert, and I want to make your day better. Let me help you."

o A video supplement. Videos change up the talk and recapture audience attention. Make sure that the video doesn't take away from the presentation, but actually adds to the point that you're trying to make. Just remember that three- or four-minute-long videos are good. A twenty-minute video is too long, and signals to the audience that the speaker was poorly prepared.

• If speaking is important enough to your career, this could be a matter where you hire a professional to help you learn to do what you have to do: to learn how to give a presentation or a sales talk. Do you remember the movie The King's Speech? It's about King George IV of Great Britain, who had to give a historically important speech as his country went to war. It was based on a true story. His speech impediment was a glaring problem, and the speaking coach helped him overcome and give an impassioned speech that inspired the people of Great Britain as they entered World War II against a terrifying enemy.

Here's an exercise to help overcome the fear of public speaking and getting more out of your head and into your heart.

EDGY EXERCISE #2

You will need a small group for this. Put these 10 things on sheets of paper and put them in a bowl for a drawing. Take turns getting up in front of the group and acting out. This will also work virtually via Zoom, Facebook Live, or other software. The host can private message the speaker their topic, and the speaker only has 30 seconds to prepare their talk in their mind and 60 seconds to deliver it. Some examples are (and you can modify it based on your group, location, group interests and demographics, etc....)

1. Tell/show us how to change the oil in a car.

2. Tell/show us how to fly a kite.

3. Tell/show us how to make a bottle of formula and feed a baby.

4. Tell/show us how to forecast the weather.

5. Tell/show us how to bait a hook and catch a fish.

6. Tell/show us how to wash your car.

7. Tell/show us how to snow ski.

8. Tell/show us how to train for a marathon.

9. Tell/show us how to fall in love.

10. Tell/show us how to prepare a meal for ten people.

CONFIDENCE IS KEY

I think confidence, alone, could make a huge difference in the way you enter a room and the way you participate in that room. You see, overcoming the fear of public speaking is not up to your audience; it's up to you. It's all about the conversations you're having in your own head. It's about the insecurities in your own heart and mind. But once you center on the fact that you are worthy, you do matter, and your message is important—even life-changing, then your paradigm begins to shift.

You begin to realize, "It would be so selfish of me NOT to deliver this life-changing message to my audience."

GET OVER YOURSELF

When you realize that over-obsessing over the way you look, the way you sound, and how you are accepted by an audience is selfish, egotistical, and even narcissistic, you can begin to see, serve, and sow into others.

Once we begin to "get over ourselves", we can truly become the conduit we were born to be.

It's not that we don't dress well, groom well, and shave well, but that's only a part of it. Preparation on the outside can never equal preparation on the inside. And remember, it's not just the hours of preparation you're putting into this upcoming keynote. It's the lifetime of preparation that has gotten you to this moment in your career and qualified you to make this maximum impact. This makes you worth $5,000, $10,000, or even $15,000 an hour or more.

EXERCISE YOUR "MUSCLE" OF SPEECH

Your ability as a public speaker will increase every time you do it. Just like hitting the gym frequently, hitting the stage frequently has its benefits, if you take it seriously. Over time, your effectiveness, influence, and impact will grow, along with your hourly retail rate and the number of testimonials.

I've been coaching speakers for 30 years, and I was surprised to learn how many of the top paid speakers in the world are actually shy and introverted. Watch some of the top speakers with the most views of their Ted Talk, and you'll see it, too. My question to you is if some of the world's top paid speakers can be effective platform communicators, can't you, too?

EDGY EXERCISE #3

Exercises to Grow Your Speaking Skills

1. Strike up conversations with random strangers at the grocery store and other places.

2. Work on becoming a better listener by consciously pausing and taking a breath when the other person is done and asking them, "Is there more?"

3. Find a mentor and share your strengths verbally. "I'm good at x, y, and z…" Learn to be strong, vocal, and confident with what you are good at.

The more you speak, the better you get. Maybe you were told to be quiet as a child and not to speak unless spoken to? No doubt, silence does have value, but only when you are thinking or listening. Your voice is needed and missing in the world. I want you to get very comfortable in your own voice and on the stage and in the interview chair. The more comfortable you are speaking with your voice from your heart, clearly stating what you need and want, the better your audience will respond, the more effective you will be, and you'll take home a much fatter paycheck and get invited back again and again!

Chapter 6
IDENTIFY YOUR SPACE

THE FIRST STEP IN BECOMING THE NEXT ICONIC LEADER IN YOUR SPACE IS TO IDENTIFY WHO THE MAJOR INFLUENCERS ARE IN THAT SPACE NOW

Humans make a buying decision at a sub-conscious level within seven seconds of us opening our mouth, which shows that speaking is not just verbal. In fact, your audience will remember only 15 percent of what you say, because 85 percent of communication is non-verbal.

Before we can get into the mechanics of a good speech, we need to address the package. Since your audience is going to make a subconscious judgment about you within the first seven seconds of your speech, it's important to be packaged properly. And if you don't like to be the fish in the fishbowl that everyone is staring at and judging for 50 minutes, perhaps a career as a public speaker is not for you. And let's face it – despite the fact that with the right training and coaching, presumably lots of people could make a career in public speaking, very few ever do. It requires a certain amount of determination, a desire to truly be heard, and a trust from within yourself that what you have to say is of real value.

FINDING YOUR STYLE

The first – and most important – rule of finding your style is BE YOU. The world does not want you imitating someone else.

When it comes to finding YOUR voice, it's important that it's your voice and not someone else's voice. You only discover YOUR voice when you do a deep dive into your heart and soul and discover the divine thumbprint of God on the inside of you, programmed into your DNA before you were born. There is a word, there is a voice, there is a sound that is so uniquely yours that no one else can deliver.

You might have a favorite speaker you like to listen to, others you admire, or have saved as favorites on your podcast, or make a point to watch on YouTube, because their content, style, delivery, and methods speak to you. And sure, it's okay to study them, as well as the great speakers and orators throughout history for inspiration, learning, and context, but mimicking someone else's style or delivery will not give you the same results. You must ask yourself, "What is my message?"

What is the message you were born to deliver to this world?

CHOOSING A LANE: SPEAKING BASED ON YOUR CURRENT EXPERTISE

It should go without saying that if you're going to be a highly paid professional speaker, you need to know something about your topic.

What is your lane? Where is your expertise? What is

your degree in? What have you been doing for the past 20 years? You have certain qualifications, training, education, skillsets, proprietary knowledge, and experiences that make you uniquely qualified—what is that topic? Is there demand for the topic? Is this topic space over-crowded? Are event planners looking for speakers with your expertise and keynote?

Perhaps you speak on:

- Corporate culture
- Diversity and inclusion
- Employee retention and engagement
- Customer service
- Sales and sales training
- Motivational and inspirational Leadership (sharing your story)
- Time management
- Technology
- Artificial intelligence
- Virtual reality
- Augmented reality

By identifying where your target topic will land in the overall choice of topics, you can drill down and decide if you need a narrower focus within your niche, or if broad and general is sufficient. For example, if you're speaking on artificial intelligence, depending on your audience, you may need to give a foundation of context before you dive into the technical aspects of A.I., so your audience understands the industry and where it's headed to be able to grasp your content more easily.

WHAT ARE YOU GREAT AT?

Every effective speaker must "pick a lane," and pick one early to succeed and be most effective in public speaking. For example, if I'm a Certified Financial Planner (CFP) and my goal is to gain more clients with my speaking, I'm obviously going to be well-served to have a keynote and a workshop on the topics of wealth and money. I would craft my signature talk around these topics. The fastest way to dilute my brand would be to advertise that I also speak about relationships, marriage, and interpersonal communication.

The more laser-focused a speaker can be with their signature talk, the more effective that speaker can be in gaining new clients, getting invited back to speak, and expanding their online brand footprint.

In public speaking, you want to be known for one keynote speech, at the most two. What is your signature keynote talk? What is your brand? Do you speak about relationships? Do you keynote about money? Are you the credit repair guru? Is your talk about diversity and inclusion, employee engagement, employee retention, corporate culture, customer services, motivation, sales training, inspiration, or political talk? Are you a veteran and share about overcoming tragedy? Are you an athlete or politician or pastor sharing your story and your book? Are you a comedian, entertainer, or astronaut? Are you a tech guru sharing about your IPO, going public, your successful exit, or the future of tech?

WHO IS YOUR AUDIENCE? SPEAKING BASED ON WHO YOU'RE SPEAKING TO

Often, the answer to the question "What is my topic?" is "It depends on who your customer is!"

Who is your customer? How can you generate leads in your desired customer base, to increase referrals?

My first book was called *The Single Dad's Survival Guide*. That wasn't going to be my premiere topic and definitely not my overall brand. It's a part of my brand, because I had both gone through a divorce and started a publishing company. I realized that while there were many resources for single moms, there really weren't a lot of resources for single dads. So, I wrote a book on it. As a result, I was invited to speak on podcasts, and I was invited to seminars, workshops, and conferences.

Meanwhile, I also spoke in other places about how to write and publish a book, how to get best-seller status with a book, and so on. I also went into the faith community to do conferences there with my nonprofit.

YOUR SPEECH DEPENDS ON WHO YOUR CUSTOMER IS

It might be something that you know from experience, or it might be a message that is burning in your heart, something you are passionate about that has grown into an online community.

Recently, I bought a new house. I loved working with my realtor, because it saved me a lot of time. My realtor was very smart, because when it comes to finding new customers for the realtor, most of his new customers come through referrals, but a lot of them come through SEO (search engine optimization) and Google searches. If I am a real estate agent and I want to represent buyers and sellers, I want to be perceived as an expert in that space. So, I may do a free seminar online about how to improve or repair your credit. Because I've got people who want to buy a house right now, but they're not ready with their credit and their savings. I might take them down the path that leads to home ownership by this time next year. Or maybe I teach you how to stage your home, so it sells faster. On my social media, I would have videos showing these things. I'll have speaking topics around the things that feed my primary income.

Who Do You Admire?

Speaking Based on Where You Want to Go

This is picking a topic based on where you are going. Perhaps you want to be the next Suze Orman or Dave Ramsey speaking on the topic of money. As a financial planner, there are steps to take to make the jump from local financial planner to celebrity status national icon.

One of the best ways to make yourself a better public speaker in sales is in the network marketing and direct sales space.

COMPLIANCE IN SPEAKING

Compliance is a big deal when speaking. Some industries are more compliance-heavy than others. Industries like medical, legal, raising capital, and others are strictly regulated by the FDA, FTC, FCC, and the American Bar Association.

It's important for you, as the professional speaker in your industry, to be keenly aware of the laws in your state and in the nation, what they are now and what the new laws are. There are civil and criminal penalties along with fines and even jail time if you don't comply.

Chapter 7
PREPARING YOUR PRESENTATION

"HOW LONG DID YOU PREPARE FOR THIS TALK?" IS A FREQUENT QUESTION YOU WILL BE ASKED AS A HIGHLY PAID, FULL-TIME PROFESSIONAL SPEAKER"

The answer is, "I've been preparing my entire life."

And it's true. It's not just the four to six hours you prepared for this keynote. It's the lifetime of experience, heart, and soul you bring to the stage and to every talk. It's important to live in a state of readiness. When your number is called, you are ready to take the stage and do the job many others aren't willing to do.

WRITING YOUR PRESENTATION

Very much like making a recipe in the kitchen, a speech contains a certain number of ingredients in a format that anyone presumably can follow. But it's the way you prepare those ingredients and the way you present them that determines how good that "dish" is going to be. How much of an impact can you make?

These are the basic parts of a presentation and the glue that holds them together:

- The Introduction: What is it that you're going to teach the audience? Start with a statistic or story to grab the audience's attention. Further establish your credibility. Always make it about the audience, and tell them what you're going to be serving over the next 45 minutes, so they don't check out. You want them plugged into you. Be very specific about what they have to gain by listening to you.

- The Body: Tell them the information. This is the brick and mortar, the meat of your talk.

- The Conclusion: Let your audience know what they have learned from you. Drive the point home strongly and make a call to action.

- The Transitions: A transition should segue one part of your speech into the next without being clunky, but they also serve to keep the audience watching you. Attention spans wander if you don't draw them back to you, but almost any change will do the trick. Switch up the tone of your voice, your position on stage, your visual aids, start some music, tell a joke, just use your imagination.

- Storytelling: This will keep the audience engaged and help them identify with you.

PRACTICE MAKES PERFECT

Speaking takes practice. You don't get great overnight. I can remember the hours in the backyard on the farm in Oklahoma, playing catch, first with my dad and then with my brother. Catching and throwing and throwing and catching. Throwing and catching for hours. Those are some of my best memories. Apart from great conversations about life, it was something that soon would become second nature, you could almost do it in your sleep and with your eyes closed. It would later prove to help me and my brother when we had just eight players at our championship game in little league– normally, baseball has nine players on the field at once, but one of the boys quit. This put our team at a disadvantage, because every time this ninth player was "up to bat" we had a forced "ghost out". Because of the countless hours of practice in the backyard, with my brother as catcher, and me as second baseman, I don't remember a time we let a runner "steal" second base. We always got him out at second.

DON'T PRACTICE ON YOUR FAMILY

I don't recommend practicing your public speaking on your family. It can be downright disheartening and discouraging. Either they won't give you honest feedback because they don't want to hurt your feelings, or they will crush you with their criticism and not see the potential in you. Very few family members can help you with this. It's better to go to your business professional peers. You can find groups on Facebook and develop a friendship and ask for feedback. You can even hire someone on Fiverr.com for $5 to practice on Zoom with, if you want a total stranger.

One of my favorite groups to sharpen your public speaking skills is Toastmasters. They have chapters all over the world, they have a proven system, and it's free.

You will get honest and objective feedback, and these peers will be some of your best friends in your speaking career. Some of the great speakers of our generation have come through Toastmasters, including Les Brown and Darren LaCroix.

CHECKING THE ROOM

It's always a good idea to tour the venue where you'll be speaking. This is why you'll want to arrive early as often as possible. Organize with your event host to fly in the day before, if possible, and look at the meeting room. This will help you explore the room and preview the logistics and go through your checklists (see Chapter Thirteen: Resources for checklists). This will also help you visualize success as you run through your speech a final time in your hotel room the night before.

If you're traveling internationally, I would recommend talking to your event host first to see if there are any cultural or religious faux pas that you want to avoid, any hand gestures or words or greetings that may be commonplace in your country, but because this is a different part of the world, you want to be careful about these things.

Chapter 8
DELIVERING THE PRESENTATION

The big day has finally arrived! It is time for your presentation! There are a few things you'll want to do to ensure success.

DRESS FOR SUCCESS

When speaking before an audience, you want to be well-groomed, professional, and one level above your audience's attire. Don't wear ill-fitting clothes – the number one fashion mistake you can make is wearing clothes that don't fit you. High-paying speaking gigs demand that you look the part, like you belong in the room. If you are on a budget, clothing "looks" can be changed up by accessorizing, switching ties, jackets, etc.

Dress yourself like you're interviewing for a job you really want, and groom yourself like you're going on date with someone you truly want to impress. That means a manicure, tamed eyebrows, trimmed nose and ear hairs, clean teeth, and clean hair in a good haircut.

Consider your audience when you dress yourself. Consider who you want them to see on stage. If you're especially talented in assessing your clothing and appearance, enlist some real-life help or read up on the subject, because first impressions are exactly as important as you've always believed.

PICKING THE RIGHT PERSON TO INTRODUCE YOU

Third-party credibility is huge in the speaking industry. Without it, you have nothing. Third-party credibility establishes perceived value in the marketplace. Once the event is on the calendar, ask the event host if he/she has someone who normally does the introductions of guest speakers.

This could be someone who is normally an emcee, a moderator, or a speaker themselves. You want someone who is confident, firm, outspoken, and not afraid to be on stage. They are going to "set the stage" and bring you up properly. You will provide a short bio, not the long one. The long one belongs on your website. A short one of 400 to 500 words maximum is sufficient. It should end with".... *please get on your feet and put your hands together and help me welcome (your name) to the stage!"*

The other thing you want to ask your announcer to do is to have the event attendees move in closer to the front. This will give you, as a speaker, a better connection with your audience and will render better photos of you speaking from stage. A half full room of attendees looks much better when they are in the front half of the room.

VISUALIZING SUCCESS

The success of any speech or talk is determined by the goals established with the event host prior to the event. What is the goal of your keynote? Is it to motivate? Inspire? Educate? Train? Entertain? What is the call to action? What action do you want your audience to take to at the end of your talk? You'll want to visualize this success in your mind before speaking. You'll want to imagine yourself taking the stage and winning over the audience with your message and imagine a standing ovation. By doing this rehearsal in your mind, you will be much more prepared to actually give the talk in real life, and will be much calmer and more at ease.

GETTING PHOTOS/VIDEOS OF YOU SPEAKING AT YOUR EVENT

You will want to make sure you get photos and videos of your speaking engagements to use on social media as proof that you actually are a speaker in a professional setting, and that you do, in fact, have customers and clients, and that people receive input and positivity from your talks. I'm sharing our speaker contract with you. You will notice that the approval for photos and videos is a part of that contract. You'll want approval ahead of time, so there are no surprises!

FOLLOW-UP AFTER THE PRESENTATION / GETTING INVITED BACK

Use a speaker survey sheet, either a paper survey or an online survey, which will give you feedback for the event from your host on ways you can improve, how the talk was received, and any other feedback the promoter received from the audience. Speakers who show that they care about results are invited back. This level of interest confirms that you care about the audience and the host.

Chapter 9
BRANDING AND MARKETING YOURSELF

THE VOICE IN YOUR HEART, SPEAKING TO YOUR HEAD EVERY DAY, TRYING TO GET YOU TO TAKE ACTION IN THE DIRECTION OF YOUR DESTINY, THAT IS THE VOICE THE WORLD DESPERATELY NEEDS TO HEAR!

If you're going to be a speaker on any topic, in any industry, my recommendation is to start online first. As we'll discuss in the chapter on networking, beginning online seriously mitigates the financial risks you must take to become a known public speaker.

But establishing yourself online requires branding. When you google your keywords, what comes up? Who are the paid professional speakers right now that are already speaking in your target market? That's what you want. You want to come up on the first page of Google, because we all know that most people never make to the second, much less the third page of Google. There is a reason there is so much competition to get at the top of organic Google searches. That's where you want to be. That won't happen unless you have the social media around your brand and around your keywords.

This is exactly why I include this topic in my Speak Better in 60 Days seminar, where I and my team help speakers learn about SEO, keywords, and what needs to happen next, to really get "found" on the marketing side of online speaking.

WHAT DOES IT MEAN TO "BRAND" YOURSELF?

For a long time, I thought branding was the smell of singed hair and the squeal of an angry, 500-pound young heifer as the Rocking B Ranch logo was permanently seared into her backside. That memory is so embedded in my brain, it's almost as if I'm still there, hearing my grandfather tell that story to me and my brother 1,158 times. It had become my memory. It was a part of me. "That's right son," Grandpa had said, "that was before we had fences. We all used to brand our cattle, so they couldn't get lost or easily stolen, and you would know which T-bone steak to buy from the butcher."

Branding now means something completely different, and it's something you must do in order to make space for yourself in the crowded room of the public speaking world. It begins with your website. Branding is perception. Ninety percent of effective branding is visual. Yes, the words are important, but the selfies you take to the pictures you post to the way you pose for a photo and even the angle you point your chin and the way you smile all become a part of your brand.

Authentic branding is bigger than a logo, haircut, prop a wardrobe a car or a backdrop at a photo shoot; it is your core life message, your core values you hold personally and as a company. It is the way you treat your customers; it is the reviews your customers leave on your Yelp, Google, and Facebook.

Remember the Yellow Pages? Every year, you'd have two to three bulky yellow directories land on the front porch of your home or business. It was important for business because, pre-internet, before we had Google, people would actually search for a plumber, an electrician, or a heating and air person in the Yellow Pages.

So, in order for people to easily find their business first, many companies named themselves with as many letter "A"s as they could manage (AAA Taxi, AAA Automotive, AAA Pest Control), because they wanted to show up on the first page of the alphabetically organized Yellow Pages. Since we now use Google and the Internet, we don't need AAA on our businesses in order to be found online, but we do need a branding and marketing strategy that works. *Before someone hires you to speak, they scroll through your social media. Make certain that your social media matches the brand you want to convey.*

The way you dress in public is your brand, the car you drive is your brand, and your house is a part of your brand. I understand you might not be able to have the best house and car you would like, but if you're going to do a Zoom or a Facebook Live from home, get organized and tidy up your office.

If you're selling financial services, you want to build the brand accordingly. It doesn't mean you have to have

Lamborghinis and Ferraris in all of your posts, but maybe you do in some, if that's who you're targeting. If you're speaking on health and nutrition, you want your photos and your social media to portray that brand.

If I'm a CFP and my signature talk is on wealth, then it makes sense for me to build my brand around that. I might also have a workshop on credit repair or even a stand-alone keynote I can do for stages, or a podcast on improving your credit in spite of personal and national economic downturns. This topic runs parallel and congruently to my brand, and so it works.

Illustrating another industry, as a health practitioner, a doctor, health coach, nurse, or wellness consultant, perhaps your primary speaking topic is "Natural Wellness in the Pharmaceutical Age" and you focus on weight management, nutrition, exercise, and longevity. It makes sense to have a workshop on "Diabetes Prevention", "Stroke Detection", "Immune System Boosting", etc.— even "Sexual Health for the Aging". You want to be known as The Wellness Coach or The Health Guru or The Doctor's Corner, etc. You might begin to engage your customers with a free health assessment. In return for their giving you their email address for a free health assessment, they watch a five-minute video where you give an overview. Then you want to set up the appointment, so you can get them signed up for your program or for your product.

Of course, in your book or in your seminars, you are free to talk about other subjects, but never do so at the risk of diluting your primary brand.

WHAT THREE-WORD MONIKER FITS YOUR BRAND?

Naming your personal brand is just as important as naming a brick-and-mortar business. It helps humans quickly learn who you are and know how to refer you. It helps customers discover you in searches, with search engine optimization (SEO). Since humans and other business owners who may want to hire you have a short attention span, the quickest way for your networking and introductions to turn into business is for someone to quickly know what it is you do and how they can refer you.

Describe who you are and what you can do in three words. Here are some examples:

- Credit Repair Strategist- Long-Term and Short-Term Credit Repair Solutions

- Optimal Health Catalyst – Assessing, Planning, and Executing Your Health Goals

- Business Start-up Strategist – Helping You Launch Your Next Business

- Fitness Health Coach – Getting You Healthy

- Ergo Efficiency Optimizer – Helping You Maximize Your Space at Home and at the Office
- The Alchemy Architect – Done-for-You Systems for Entrepreneurs to Monetize Their Tribe for Life

CONTINUING EDUCATION

Every industry requires continuing education to be successful in that industry. Some industries require it, and you can't continue to work in and get paid in that industry unless you have so many hours of verified continuing education. The same should be true for Speaking Professionals from the beginner to the Certified Speaking Professional (CSP).

Personally, I like to listen to a wide variety of speakers in multiple industries, but I do have my favorite go-to speakers for motivation, education, information, faith, and technology. Remember, who you listen to today is who you will be tomorrow. Who you spend time with now will be the direction your life is headed.

OWNING THE INDUSTRY

As a professional speaker, you can have one or two good keynotes that wow the audiences, but if you're not constantly reading, growing and learning, you'll lose the edge in a short amount of time, and it will be noticeable, both to the experts in your industry and those who have hired you in the past. "He says the same thing every time," they will say. "Why bother with this speaker? We want someone with something new to say."

Les Brown is considered one of the world's greatest speakers. He got his start in radio and went on to win the Golden Gavel in Toastmasters as their top speaker. He says he gave many free speeches before ever getting paid for a speech, but he said he put just as much effort, research, and study into those free speeches and says that's how he started getting paid speaking events. And even after being one of the top paid speakers in the world, getting $75,000 per speech, he still puts in hours of research for each speech and customizes it for the individual company, organization, or group he's speaking to. You might hear some of the same stories, but he will drive the point home from a different angle based on who his crowd is and what the event organizer has told him the organization is going through right now. This has earned him the title as one of the top 10 speakers in the world.

THE SPEAKER "SIZZLE REEL"

When event planners and COOs hire you for a speaking event, conference, meeting, or workshop, they want to see a two-minute speaker sizzle reel on your website. They want to see you doing your thing and see what others are saying about you. You will want to have this professionally produced. Potential customers will find it difficult to take you seriously if it doesn't look like you take yourself seriously. Your cousin or nephew might be "pretty good" at video production, but if it looks homemade, you won't get the call.

Anything longer than two minutes is too long. They just want to "test drive you" by seeing you on stage and what others are saying about you. It's better to have four to five short videos than one long one. Have your sizzle reel as the main feature and additional testimonial videos ("what others are saying") below your sizzle reel for maximum impact.

Chapter 10
SELLING FROM STAGE

Selling from stage is an art. Selling from stage is a craft. It takes skill, strategic finesse, and incredible trust. Es-tablishing rapport with your audience is the first thing a speaker needs to do. Sales resistance is high, because many people in your audience have been burned—you are not the first to try to sell them something from stage. The true masters of selling from stage can sell to you without you ever being aware that is what they are do-ing. Instead, what they hear is someone offering them a solution they have been seeking.

How do you approach a sale without it feeling like a sale? It's really focusing on what the customers want. Asking a series of questions, then listening carefully to their answers, will help you determine the best way to get what they want.

There is really no difference between selling to an audience and selling to an individual. It's always about es-tablishing trust and being transparent and authentic. If I am a car salesman, I tell the customer, "All of our prices are marked on the window. We don't negotiate or haggle; that's our rock-bottom price for you." Then, they know exactly what to expect.

I'm going to be empathetic. I'm going to ask questions. I'm going to tell a story. "Tom was in here last week, he brought in a car about like yours, and here's what we did for him on the trade-in. Kind of like you, he had a new baby," and so on.

Getting the sale is a series of "yes" answers and estab-lishing trust. You can tell the customer, "Hey, I might not be able to help you today, but if you decide you see something you want, or if you decide not to do business with me today, that's okay." And it is okay for the cus-tomer to say no, but they are going to say "yes" or "no" before they leave here today.

So, in other words, I'm conditioning them that saying, "I'm thinking it over," is not going to cut it. In the same way, I'm telling an audience, "Okay, you're either going to say 'yes, you're going to accept the timeshare presenta-tion' or 'no, you're not interested.'"

ESTABLISHING THE "KNOW, LIKE, AND TRUST" FACTOR

Speaking on stage requires the "know, like and trust" factor. This is why it's important to personalize some illus-trations and establish credibility when taking the stage. Third-party credibility can be established through the em-cee with your bio, playing your sizzle reel, or both. This can show which clients you have worked with – just make sure it's not a competitor to the company or audience you're speaking with! Particularly if you're selling from stage, there has to be a great level of trust, because you're asking your audience to take action. Perhaps you're not trying to sell a particular product, but never-theless, you are still selling yourself and your ideas. You do want them to listen to your keynote, then take your call-to-action to heart, and take the next steps.

If you've given value from the moment you've been on stage, you can get someone to buy pretty much any-thing from you. You've connected from a heart level. They've heard your stories, they've seen you cry, and they have maybe even shed a few tears with you or at least opened their heart a bit. Now's your chance to bring them further into the relationship with you and your business.

OVERCOMING OBJECTIONS

Overcoming objections is something that all salespeople deal with. It's a part of their training and lingo. Rebut-tals are resistance to the sales process when someone is on your doorstep or on your phone trying to sell you something.

They're really objecting to the fact that they don't want to be taken advantage of or give up their money. They know they need a new car, but they're afraid they will re-gret the purchase, overcommit, or be swindled somehow. As a salesperson, I'm listening for those things. The best way to communicate is to listen for what those objections are. What are their concerns? Listen for signs of the way they think. Left brain or right brain? Creative-minded or engineer-minded? Know how to give the facts to certain personality types that will help them make a decision. If I know that the husband is going to be emotional and the wife is going to be logical or vice versa, I use that to my advantage to give them the car that they want. Because they came there, they want a car. I'm going to do a good job by educating them and selling them the car that they want. It's a win/win, and I have communicated effectively based on their communication style.

Chapter 11

GENERATING SPEAKING ENGAGEMENTS

How many public speaking events do you want to have this year?

WHY I RECOMMEND STARTING ONLINE

Committing to filling an auditorium or a banquet hall is a big financial investment and involves a lot of risk. In the past, I've done literally hundreds of events in hotels. Making that commitment to fill that hotel ballroom, not knowing if people are going to show up...that can be scary. You have to pay event planners, entertainers, and caterers, whether or not you make a dime. It's a big deal to sweat those details, hoping to break even, maybe even make a profit.

Starting online mitigates risk. Host a free webinar, build an email list, and develop a tribe of people you communicate with regularly through social media and video communication. Build that on multiple platforms. Then, when you have a following and solid social branding, you will be ready to move on to live public performances.

LEVERAGING FREE SPEAKING EVENTS TO GET PAID SPEAKING EVENTS

Most professional speakers do give several free speeches a year as a way of giving back and paying it forward.

Speaking for free is also an excellent way to advertise your power and effectiveness as a speaker, because you never know who is sitting in the audience of a "free" speech. Pass out your business card or a brochure. Many people belong to organizations, clubs, and companies that are frequently in the market for a good speaker, or they know someone who is. Impress them, and suddenly you're a recipient of the best advertising in the world: word of mouth.

Types of Free Events. You can utilize Rotary Club and Toastmasters, faith-based events, virtual events, and Chamber of Commerce networking groups to give free speeches to let people know about their business and what kind of referrals you're looking for. It's also a great way to give a motivational speech to a civic group or an organization that needs some encouragement; it's a great way to pay it forward and let people know that even though you are speaking in other places and get-ting paid, you are doing a free speech for this non-profit group because they are a non-profit. Be sure to add that you are also available to be hired to speak, in case they're interested.

THE ELEVATOR PITCH

An elevator pitch is a thirty-to-sixty second pitch. It doesn't necessarily have to be "in an elevator", but what it means is that you should be able to tell someone what you are and what you can offer within a few brief mo-ments: about the length of an elevator ride. When you meet someone and they say, "So, what do you do?" you need to be able to respond with a confident, interesting answer. Never start a "pitch" with uncertain words like, "Well, it's hard to describe," or "I guess it depends on who's asking." Be brief, pithy, and unforgettable.

A book publisher might say, "Have you ever met someone who always hears from friends and family, 'You should write a book.' Well, I'm the person who helps them get their book out to the world. I'm a book publisher." They'll usually say, "Oh, wow! Everybody tells me I should write a book. Let me have your card." And so, it's a quick pitch.

An elevator pitch is a great networking skill for business. It allows you to quickly introduce yourself to the person you meet at church, a networking event, or even the grocery store.

HOW TO FIND PAYING SPEAKING ENGAGEMENTS

There are a number of ways to get on stage for free, but how do you get paid speaking gigs?

1. Host your own event.

2. Promote yourself as a speaker who can be found, hired, or referred by customers.

3. ay to be on someone else's stage. The event planner can let you know how many people will be in the room, and when you sell your book or your business, this is a way to make your money back. Also, people in the audience might want to pay you to come and speak at their event.

I actually prefer number 1. When I host my own events, I have the greatest potential for loss, but also the greatest potential for reward.

Back in the 90s, I filled hotel ballrooms with people in the direct sales and network marketing space. I loved being on stage. More importantly, I loved featuring my top distributors on stage. Being on stage is one thing; creating that opportunity for someone else is the ulti-mate experience!

PAYING TO BE ON SOMEONE'S VIRTUAL OR PHYSICAL STAGE

When I get on some else's stage, they are typically re-sponsible for promoting it, advertising it, and having at-tendees show up. I basically show up, speak, and sell. When I'm paying to speak on someone else's stage, it's normally a one-off investment, and I keep 100 percent of my sales or I do a revenue share with the host on the back end, and they make a certain percentage of the proceeds, like 50/50 or 60/40. Whatever you negotiate with the host, be sure you have it in writing.

SPEAKERS' BUREAUS: WHAT ARE THEY, AND ARE THEY WORTH IT?

I believe strongly in the value of speakers' bureaus. That is why I started one myself at GlobalEliteSpeakersBureau. com. A speakers' bureau is actively marketing speakers around their core topic to specific event planners. They market people who speak on certain issues to the people who are looking for those types of speakers. Whatever category: CPA associations, safety, OSHA, diversity and inclusion, corporate culture, nonprofit, AI, science and tech, stocks money and finances, relationships...the list goes on and on. There's no out-of-pocket expense to the speaker, unless and until they are booked onstage to speak.

Chapter 12
THE FUTURE OF PROFESSIONAL PUBLIC SPEAKING

THE FUTURE OF PUBLIC SPEAKING WILL BE A HYBRID OF VIRTUAL AND LIVE EVENTS

The Coronavirus has changed the speaking industry in the United States and around the world. Professional speakers who want to thrive in 2020 and beyond as viable, full-time professional speakers will need to innovate and innovate quickly.

Historically, the "market" for public speakers has gone through its own fluctuations. Many thought the speaking industry would die in 2008 with the economic crash. According to the National Speaker's Association, speaking gigs and speaking income fell by 66 percent from 2007 to 2009.

Many full-time speakers transitioned into employment and left the speaking industry entirely. The smart speakers innovated by creating online courses and doing virtual events. Many of those same speakers are thriving today because they created a business model around their speaking that included:

1. Membership websites.
2. Coaching programs.
3. Virtual events.
4. Setting up clients on retainer.

There are things new and veteran speakers can do to provide real value through the crisis, gain market share, and thrive in their respective niches.

AVERAGE SPEAKER SALARIES FOR PUBLIC SPEAKERS

According to Salary.com, the median salary for public speakers as of December of 2020 was $88,754.

The salary range for public speakers usually falls between $78,301 and $99,705. Salary ranges depend on factors like your education and skill level, your certifications, and the number of years you have been working.

The upper 10 percent of public speakers make in excess of $109,000 annually, and the lower 10 percent make less than $68,785.

Seven Things Speakers Can Do to Thrive, In Spite of the Coronavirus Pandemic:

1. Launch your podcast, or re-launch your podcast.
2. Host guests on your Zoom, Facebook Live, or your podcast.
3. Write and launch another book.
4. Turn your current or previous books into online courses.

5. Host virtual events and invite guests.

6. Create joint ventures with complementary businesses to cross-promote to each other's lists.

7. Develop and launch a high-end Master-Mind coaching program.

Chapter 13
RESOURCES

The fact is, at some time or another, and especially at work, almost everyone will be called upon to speak. In some jobs, it is essential. That is what I'm here to help you with. I want to give you the tools in eight days or less to be a powerful public speaker.

Better speaking adds value to your bottom line and your bank account. You'll attract better customers and retain them longer – better yet, they will become their referral partners.

SPEAKBETTER60DAYS.COM

Speak Better 60 Days is an eight-part seminar I conduct, available online. It is my 35 years of experience teaching public speaking around the world condensed into eight hours, and depending on your determination, you can finish the program in eight weeks, eight days, or in one day. The course teaches all of the following, and more:

1. Overcoming fear.

2. Finding your topic.

3. Impromptu speaking.

4. Closing the sale from the stage.

5. Practical mechanics: hand gestures, tone, pitch, etc.

6. The five must-haves and the five can't-stands of any audience.

7. How to find event planners.

8. The business of public speaking.

9. Is a speakers' bureau right for you?

10. How do you sell yourself as a speaker?

11. International speaking.

12. Corporate stages.

13. Non-profit stages.

14. What topics pay the most in the various sectors?

15. How do you build your own successful online speaking course?

16. How to host your own event.

For more resources and current speaking tips go to: **SpeakBetter60Days.com**

ABOUT THE AUTHOR

MICHAEL D. BUTLER
DALLAS, TX

Like you, Michael D. Butler has been speaking all his life – but for a time, speaking was the most difficult and stressful part of his world. Butler stuttered as a child from age 5 to age 11, and although naturally outgoing and gregarious, the social stigma from this impediment caused him to withdraw. To cope with isolation, he became imaginative and creative... maybe a little too creative.

Butler remembers sitting in the principal's office in second grade, only seven years old, and sincerely believing that he was about to be sent to reform school. It was the twelfth time his parents had been called to speak to the school's principal about his bad behavior. This time? He was throwing rocks through classroom windows on the playground at recess. He just liked the sound the breaking glass made when the glass shattered on the inside of the classroom.

And so, he was told that reform school awaited him: the terrible food, the hard, cold beds, and the brutally mean bullies all around. No friends allowed, no play, and all work. That image made Butler certain he never wanted to go to reform school, and he made a decision to turn over a new leaf and stop causing trouble at school. No more fighting, breaking windows, or putting soap into kids' milk in the lunchroom anymore.

But Butler didn't find his voice until age 12, doing a speech for his English class on meteorology. Butler was enamored with Ronald Reagan, the "Great Communicator". His entire seventh grade class once wrote notes to Ronald Reagan; Reagan wrote back thanking them for the support. Later, with the help of a speech therapist, he emerged from his cave and discovered great pleasure in being the class clown and the life of the party.

Butler launched his entrepreneurial career at 15 when an ad he ran in the newspaper for lawn mowing got him 14 customers. Not old enough to drive, he had to hire a driver to make sure his customers got serviced. He later sold that business and went on to start a janitorial company which grew to $1 million in annual revenue in the first year. Butler would later sell that company to find his passion in the direct sales space. Training his sales teams to write a book, adopt a non-profit, and speak on stage, the natural next step was to start a social media marketing firm, which he did.

After Bible College, Butler loved the Pastoral work of the ministry for a decade-and-a-half. Being a people person and a natural story-teller, Butler loved the travel side of the ministry and spoke to 3,000 audiences in many states and multiple continents.

Michael had already been married, had four sons, and been a fulltime pastor for fourteen years when he returned to college to take advanced public speaking. He was considering transferring his hours from psychology and counseling into a degree for licensed family therapist. However, after sitting in a college classroom for one semester, he realized that "sitting still" was not for him – but being in front of a crowd, starting businesses, and launching others into success certainly was. This was the seed of the idea that led to Beyond Publishing.

Before anyone was on Facebook, Butler and his teams supporting authors and book launches were marketing their team members on MySpace. In 2010, they had their first author get a movie deal, and they knew they were on to something. Fast forward to 2020 and 14 short film festival awards later, Butler still believes in the dream and inspiring the dream in others who have a story to tell the world.

After starting Beyond Publishing, his team has published over 500 titles by 150 authors in over a dozen countries. His podcast The Publisher Podcast features guests from Hollywood and the Literary World about all things publishing. Butler runs the Global Elite Speakers Bureau that puts authors on stages globally. His non-profit rescues kids from slavery at 1040impact.org.

Butler has been a guest on Fox News and has gotten his clients onto CNN, Dr. Phil, TMZ, TLC, Rolling Stone, Entrepreneur Magazine, Inc500, TBN, TruTV, Fox Business, and many others.

He is a board member of The WorldWomenConference. com, Empowering Through Education, and The Ellamo Foundation, founded by filmmaker Manely Ellamo. His podcast ThePublisherPodcast.com can be heard on Apple Podcasts and other platforms where he does a deep dive with guests from the Literary and Hollywood world on storytelling, writing books, screenplays and getting movie deals.

He is the best-selling Author of *The Single Dad's Survival Guide, Best-Seller Status, The Speaker's Edge, It's Complicated,* and Freedom the Book, translated into multiple languages.

Butler lives in and runs his companies from Dallas, TX.

MichaelDButler.com

1040Impact.org

BeyondPublishing.net

GlobalEliteSpeakersBureau.com

As the CEO of The Mark Victor Hansen Library with over 80 New York Times Bestselling books, global distribution and sales at over half a billion books, his authors have spoken in fifty countries on six continents but he's most proud of his four grown sons and two grandsons.

LAUNCHING EVERYWHERE
Spring 2021

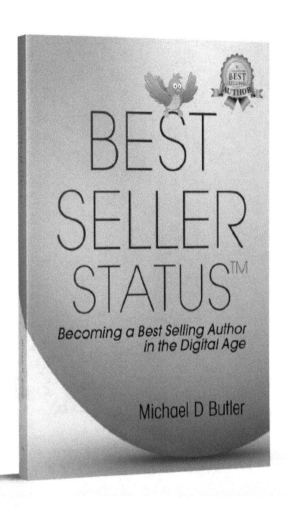

Get the book that has helped thousands write
their own best-seller!

Know a dad going through a divorce? This is the #1 resource for Single Dads - grab it now!

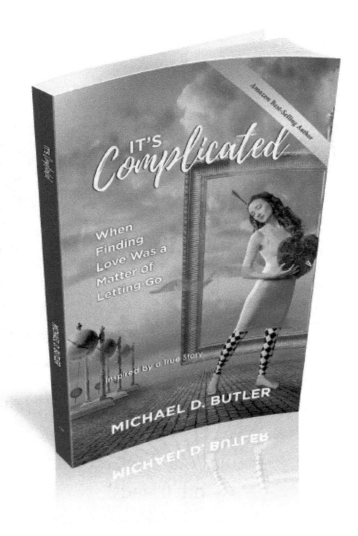

Discover
DATING, LOVE and ROMANCE
all over again!

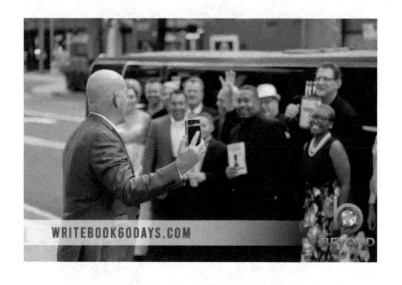

WRITEBOOK60DAYS.COM

Are you stuck trying to write your book?

Writing Your Book is better
with friends!

Are you Ready to take the Stage?
GlobalEliteSpeakersBureau.com

CPSIA information can be obtained
at www.ICGtesting.com
Printed in the USA
BVHW050451081221
623423BV00002BA/170

9 781637 921722